Giles Pease

Who is on the Lord's Side?

Or, does the Bible sanction slavery?

Giles Pease

Who is on the Lord's Side?
Or, does the Bible sanction slavery?

ISBN/EAN: 9783337243166

Printed in Europe, USA, Canada, Australia, Japan

Cover: Foto ©Lupo / pixelio.de

More available books at **www.hansebooks.com**

"WHO IS ON THE LORD'S SIDE?"

OR,

DOES THE BIBLE SANCTION SLAVERY?

BEING

AN EXAMINATION

INTO THE

EGYPTIAN, MOSAIC, AND AMERICAN

Systems of Service and Labor.

BY

GILES PEASE.

———

BOSTON:
PUBLISHED BY HENRY HOYT,
No. 9 CORNHILL.
1864.

NOTE. — The *substance* of this treatise was originally delivered, by *appointment*, before the Conference of Churches of Barnstable, Nantucket, and Dukes Counties, at Edgartown, Mass., June 13, 1854. It was subsequently delivered, as an oration, on the Fourth of July, and afterwards on the Sabbath, in two discourses.

It is now published at the solicitation of friends of liberty.

BOSTON, Sept. 22, 1864.

EGYPTIAN, MOSAIC, AND AMERICAN

SYSTEMS OF SERVICE AND LABOR

COMPARED.

"WHO IS ON THE LORD'S SIDE?"—Exo. xxxii. 26.

SINCE the first apostasy of our race,—a period of nearly six thousand years,—this world has exhibited an unremitting scene of conflict. Its history has been the history of opposing moral forces.

At the head, as leaders, of these antagonistic moral forces, are God and Satan.

Under the leadership of the one or the other,—of God or Satan,—must be ranged every individual of the human family. There can be no neutrality of position on any question affecting moral relations and moral obligations. There is no neutral ground to occupy. The cause and interest of God and Satan are never coincident. They are never to be found on the same side.

On every question, therefore, involving the principles of morality and religion, it is a matter of deep interest to every individual to understand on which side his name is registered; and, next to that, to understand who are on the same side with himself, and who are registered among the forces in opposition. This principle was well understood and acted upon in the period of our American Revolution.

(3)

While, however, by a strictly true analysis, there are but *two classes* of men in the world, and two sides to every question, there are those who *seem* or *seek* to form another class. And on no subject is this more evident than in regard to SLAVERY, on which, by appointment, I am requested to address this Conference at the present time.

FIRST. There are those who *unqualifiedly* and *openly* condemn and oppose Slavery, and seek its overthrow.

SECOND. There are those who openly and unqualifiedly support and defend the institution.

Those who occupy either of these positions men know where to find.

But there is still another class, who take neither of these positions. They are a sort of would-be-go-betweens, or stand-on-both-sides men, — aiming, like those of whom Christ speaks, to serve God and Mammon ; and after the example of the Assyrio-Samaritan Jews (2 Kings xvii. 33), who " feared the Lord, and served their own gods." Characteristically, therefore, they are found on *both sides*, according to circumstances — first on this, then on that. To some their position may seem ambiguous, doubtful ; and it is not improbable that they do not know where they are themselves. They *say* they *do not like* Slavery ; and it is plain they *do not like* those who say any thing *against* it. They *say* they are *opposed* to Slavery, in *principle ;* but their *opposition,* whenever manifested, is ever and always against those who do anything to secure its overthrow. If they ever admit, in words, that Slavery is wrong, they are very careful and prompt to qualify their condemnation by apologies, either for the practice of slaveholding or for those who indulge in it. If they allow Slavery to be wrong *in the abstract,* they are very careful not to do it any harm by any act of theirs, at the ballot-box or in legislation. They are of opinion that any action upon the subject, *in opposition*, even to the extent of calm and free discussion, only increases the evils of the system. Though they admit the institution of Slavery to be *bad*, they think it vastly worse to disturb it within its present boundaries, or even to limit the extent of its growth.

This is, *unquestionably*, the position occupied, for many years, by no small portion of the people even of the Northern States. And among them have been included not a few of the membership of our churches, and of the Ministers of New England.

It seems scarcely needful to remark, that this numerous class of our confederacy, if not *exactly* in the position which the open advocates of Slavery would have them, yet are in a position *next* to as good, viz., on the line of *professed* neutrality, where a small gravitating force could jostle them sufficiently over on to their side to give them all the advantage of withdrawing their forces from aid to the opponents of the institution.

By their assistance, as might have been expected, Representatives to Congress have been elected who have been true to the position of their constituents; yielding to the entreaties, or demands, or threats of the slave power. Acting on this *both-sides* policy, they have consented to the admission of nine States to the confederacy, with the privilege of property representation, which no Northern free State is allowed — simply to gratify the very modest wishes, and answer the demands, of the Slavocracy, to maintain the balance of power in the administration of the general government.

By this very plastic, both-sides policy, the representatives of the people have voted scores of millions of dollars for the purchase of domain for Slavery's expansion

1 *

and growth, and hundreds of millions of dollars *for wars* to defend and protect its interests.

They have consented to employ the power of the National arm — the legislative, judicial, and executive — the army and the navy — as a perpetual night and day police watch over the goods and chattels of their self-appointed and would-be owners and drivers. Yea, for the *affection* they have borne to this *dear nursling* of the people, the statutes of the nation have been made to command, under threats of heaviest penalties, that in case any man or woman shall be cognizant of an instance in which the brute chattel broke forth from the womb of Slavery, into the image of a man, they must not fail, however uncongenial the duty, like the Egyptian midwives, to put such offspring immediately to death.

Would to the Lord, that the midwives appointed by our National Government, had a spark of that humanity recorded of those appointed by the kind and tender-hearted Pharaoh, to let the *self-born* offspring of the spirit of Liberty *alone* to live, as best their mother can provide them !

But this is not all.

By the aid and assistance of those who have claimed to be men of *more* than "one idea," this large class of two-sides men, who are for *Liberty and Slavery both,* the small number of open and avowed advocates of Slavery have succeeded in gaining the consent of the nation to occupy and control all their remaining territory, to the end that the principle of freedom need give itself no further care to provide for the government of the land, but that it may give itself up, quietly and forever, to the control and supervision of the patriarchs of Slavery.

By the recent Nebraska-Kansas Territory Bill, as the legitimate result of the openly avowed principles of this two-sides policy, a territory sufficient to make fifty States as large as Massachusetts, or eighty States as large as Connecticut, has been surrendered to the principles of slaveholding despotism.

The representatives of the neutral or *non-intervention* policy have quitclaimed all their right, title, and interest in that vast domain, to a faction never found to be slow to raise the flag of *intervention* in every man's interests and business, except of tyrants.

And what is of great importance for our consideration at the present time, as well as a matter of surprise, is, that these would-be-three parties, in respect to Slavery, are now, and for some time past have been, attempting to justify their respective positions by the law of God and the gospel of Jesus Christ. They attempt, and profess to be able, to show, that God occupies *just their ground;* that God is therefore with them in their respective positions.

It should be understood, however, that these different positions in respect to Slavery, so far as our own nation is concerned, have been assumed of comparatively recent date.

Before the American revolution, Slavery was regarded and denounced as a great moral and political evil by all of the American colonies. Those colonies, which are now slaveholding States, were not less earnest in their remonstrances against the action of the British government, in introducing and permitting Slavery here, than were those colonies which are now free States. All the colonies framed laws to prevent the increase of Slavery. But these laws were vetoed by the King of Great Britain. And the exercise of arbitrary power, to enlarge and perpetuate a system universally regarded as wicked and wrongful in itself, and destructive to the interests of the colonies, was one of the chief occasions of the American revolution, and so designated in the ever-memorable Declaration of American Independence.

Till subsequent to that period in our history, there was but one party to the interests of Slavery in the land, so far as the *sentiment* of the nation was involved in the institution. The abettors and defenders were *then* found all on the other side of the flood.

But since that period, the forces which then defended and supported the institution, have been transported from their eastern home, and have become so augmented on our shores, as to claim and hold a preponderance of power in the administration of the national government.

With these changes, in the combination of the civil and political elements of the nation, have come changes, both as to the ground of the assault and defence of the institution of American Slavery.

At the first, Slavery was condemned and opposed as a moral and political evil, subversive of temporal prosperity. *But legislation against it, directly,* by the general government, was opposed, on the ground, first, of the difficulty of at once breaking up a system which had become so intimately and extensively entwined into the relations of society; and, second, on the ground of forbearance towards sinners procrastinating repentance; and, third, for the sake of peace and union; and since, fourth, and *finally,* on the ground of *the divinity of the institution.*

The whole controversy on this subject has at length been reduced to the Bible argument on the question. Those who have *maintained,* as well as those who *ridiculed* " the higher law " principle of national legislation, have been alike forward to resort to the Scriptures of truth for arguments pertaining to this subject. And on this platform professing to stand, as well as on merely political considerations, while there are, *in truth*, but two parties to the issue, there are, in fact, those who have been designated as occupying three different positions, each party attempting to justify itself in its position from the word of God..

Those who *unqualifiedly condemn and seek the overthrow of Slavery*, maintain that there is nothing in the law of God, in its spirit or letter, nothing in the gospel of Jesus Christ, in its spirit or letter, which justifies or allows any element, (provision,) or principle of American Slavery.

Those who unqualifiedly *approve and uphold Slavery*, and seek its perpetuity and extension, maintain that it is a divine institution, planted, upheld, and defended both by the Mosaic law and by the gospel of Jesus Christ.

While *the third class*, always *acting* in sympathy with the oppressor rather than against him, maintain that God is with them in their position — on both sides of the institution. They admit that Slavery is bad, *but not wholly bad;* that there are some things about it to be condemned, but not the whole thing. They affirm that the *general spirit* and tenor of God's word — the Old Testament and the New — are against it, but that God has recognized the existence of the institution and relation of Slavery in the Mosaic code, and in the gospel, and has legislated in relation to it, *for its regulation, and not its annihilation*, and so has indorsed and approved of the institution.

They thus suppose and make God to be opposed to the institution *generally* and *theoretically*, but *practically* to defend and sustain it.

I know it may be a matter of great convenience to men of easy consciences, in such a position, to have a God

who can be imagined or made to stand on both sides of
Slavery, according to the tastes of his devotees ; so that
whenever they may be under the necessity or tempta-
tion to inflict numberless and nameless wrongs upon
their helpless victims, they can invoke his most gracious
protection and paternal sympathy, and have his oracles
assure them that "their matters are all good and right
with the king."

But is this the God of Christians? Is this the God
our Pilgrim fathers worshipped? Is this HE to whom
the patriots of the revolution appealed as witness to *the
rectitude of their intentions*, when they " pledged their
lives, their fortunes, and their sacred honor " to maintain the principles they avowed in their Declaration of
Independence, that all men are created free and equal,
and endowed by their Creator with inalienable rights,
among which were " life, liberty, and the pursuit of
happiness " ?

Where is the God invoked and worshipped by the
early Pilgrims? — by their honored patriot sons and
daughters of revolutionary fame? — on which side of
Slavery is He?

If Slavery is an ordinance of Jehovah, an institution
of divine appointment and approval, in vain are all the
efforts of its foes to overthrow and destroy it.

If God approves and defends it, the friends and abettors of Slavery have reason for good courage. They
have the arm of Omnipotence for their defence and their
success.

If, on the contrary, *God is on the other side*, the friends
of liberty and freedom have reason to lift up their heads
with joy, assured that God's vengeance will not sleep
forever toward those who practically deny his care and
his sympathy for the dependent creatures of his power.

The fundamental element of success in the final struggle now being entered between the friends and foes of universal liberty, is the conscious assurance, " The Lord of hosts is with *us*."

As we come to this last struggle between the elements of Despotism and Freedom, on the wide field of God's eternal truth, let us come calmly, earnestly, and intelligently to the question, —

Does the Bible sanction Slavery?

First, let us agree upon *the thing*. What *is* Slavery? In what does it *consist* ?

Let there be no strife, or waste of words, on something undefinable and undefined.

On this point there is need of special caution. Slavery has often been confounded with numerous other things, and other things have been mistaken for Slavery, and been improperly called by that name.

I take occasion, therefore, *to define the term*, in the sense in which I design to use it, and as I understand it to be legitimately and properly employed.

To make this point as clear as practicable, I remark, —

1. That the words " slavery " and " service " are not synonymous, or interchangeable terms.

Slavery involves service, but service does not necessarily involve Slavery. Any person may be subjected to labor or service to any conceivable extent, and yet be at an infinite remove from the relation and condition of a slave.

2. The terms " bondage," " bondmen," and words of like import, as used in the Scriptures, imply no elements, in condition, in common with that of Slavery.

Slavery involves bondage, but *bondage* does not necessarily involve Slavery, and, in the Mosaic records, as I shall endeavor to show, is never used as synonymous with it.

3. *Slavery* does not consist in the hard and abusive treatment of servants, whether in short-feeding, short-clothing, hard-working, or whipping, whether little or much. It may be connected with either or all of these ; but neither of these, or all of these combined, constitute Slavery. They may either or all exist where Slavery is unknown ; and instances of Slavery may exist where neither of the above-named abuses of slaves ever occur.

4. Neither does Slavery consist in restraint from the enjoyment of liberty, by being shut up within prison walls, confined with fetters and chains. Many a man has been shut up in prison, and been restrained from the exercise of liberty, who, nevertheless, in his condition and relations, in no way resembled the slave. Even those imprisoned in our institutions for crime, and bound to hard labor for years, are in no respect like the slaves in their relations, condition, or treatment.

Slavery consists in none of the elements of evil or suffering which ordinarily pertain, under civil government, to either poverty, misfortune, or crime. It involves all the evils and sufferings which flow from these relations and circumstances, but is not composed of them, nor made up by them. A state or condition of poverty, of toil, — even of toil and labor *without reward,* — of bonds, of imprisonment, of barbarous and cruel treatment — do not constitute Slavery. They may all exist, and to any extent, and yet the idea of Slavery is unreached.

Slavery involves poverty, unpaid toil, barbarous and cruel treatment ; *but these do not constitute the thing,* nor do they bear any analogy or likeness *to the principle* or *elements* of the thing.

The principle of Slavery consists in *the chattelizing of humanity — the annihilation of human relationships — the brutalization of man —* the adjudging and treating of men, made in the image of God, *like brute beasts — as articles of merchandise.*

So far as the Slave codes can do it, *they erase the imprint of rationality, and moral accountability to God, from the soul of every person enslaved.* This is its characteristic — its distinguishing element.

In confirmation and illustration of this interpretation of Slavery, I give a few brief extracts from the slave codes of several of the model slave States : —

The Louisiana code (Art. 3) says, " A slave is one who is in the power of his master, to whom he belongs ; the master may sell him, dispose of his person, his industry, his labor ; he can do nothing, possess nothing, nor acquire anything, but must belong to his master."

According to the South Carolina code, " Slaves shall be deemed, taken, reputed, and adjudged to be chattels personal, in the hands of their masters and possessors, to all intents and purposes whatsoever." Also, " All their issue and offspring, *born* and *to be born*, shall be, and they are hereby declared to be, *and remain forever hereafter*, absolute slaves, and shall follow the condition of the mother."

The *principle* of Slavery, as here developed and legally and accurately defined, is that of *property in man —* and property of no other kind, and with no other or different relations than those of brute beasts.

The slave, male and female, is perfectly under the control and at the disposal and will of the master, to be disposed of as any other article of merchandise. The idea of human relationships — as of parents and children, of husbands and wives — by the slave codes is ut-

2

terly discarded, annihilated, as well as all obligations of obedience to God and regard for his worship. In the language of another, —

" The right of man to himself is abrogated. He is another man's property. To use himself for his own good is a crime. To keep what he earns is stealing. To take his body into his own keeping is insurrection. The profit of the master is the *end* of his being, and he a mere *means* to that end, — a mere means to an end into which his interests do not enter, and of which they constitute no portion."

" The man is not robbed of his *privileges*, but of *himself*. He is not *loaded with burdens, but made a beast of burden*. His liberty is not *restrained*, but *destroyed*. His rights are not *curtailed*, but *abolished*. Slavery does not merely exact involuntary labor, but sinks the slave into a mere *implement* of labor. It does not *abridge human comforts*, but *abrogates human nature*. It despoils a rational being of *attributes*, to constitute him a thing. The attributes of humanity are denied and discarded."

This is Slavery, as defined by the legislation and jurisprudence of the slave States — the principle of property in man — the principle that *man is only property*.

And this is it, which has been defended openly and shamelessly (but it is to be hoped in most cases ignorantly) by professing Christians and Christian ministers, — by ecclesiastical bodies, North as well as South — a *principle* which gives to the master possession and control, not only of the physical energies of his slave, of his body — *but of his immortal soul — his human intelligence — his moral faculties — even his moral virtues and Christian graces.*

Who cannot see that the *body* of the slave, without

the soul, would be a mere dead carcass of no value? that if the slave had only the intellectual power of the horse, his inferiority to the horse in physical strength, would sink him below the pecuniary value of the horse, instead of his commanding, as he now does, the price of several horses?

In advertisements of slaves to be sold, or to be hired out, their intelligence, skill, honesty, sobriety, and benevolent dispositions are particularly *specified and insisted on*, as items of primary importance in establishing their value. Their *piety* is of the greatest importance as affecting their comparative worth; and a certificate of good standing in a Baptist, Methodist, Presbyterian, or some other church, will generally compensate well for the trouble and expense of procuring it.

This, in the United States of America, in the nineteenth century, is the legal relation of master and slave — a relation that regards as goods and chattels personal to all intents, constructions, and purposes whatsoever, the immortal soul of man — the image of the invisible God — the temple of the Holy Ghost — the purchase of a Redeemer's blood!

It is folly and madness for those who profess to be men of learning, or men of common sense, to represent this statement as an empty abstraction, or a rhetorical flourish. Would that it were not, what it undeniably, incontrovertibly *is*, a veritable matter-of-fact reality, acted out every day whenever and wherever a human being is claimed and held as an American slave.

And such, we are told, is a patriarchal institution! — the Mosaic system of servitude! — and the Lord is on its side!

If Thomas Jefferson had the misfortune to have been doomed, in his early days, to attendance on the ministry of one who gave such interpretations of the Mosaic law, it is no marvel, that with the deeper pencillings, by God's own hand, upon his heart, of the principles of his moral government, he rejected such a record, as unworthy of that God whose every attribute of wisdom, and justice, and benevolence were belied by such sentiments of inhumanity.

Thomas Jefferson but uttered the sentiment embodied in all the teachings of the law and of the gospel, when he said, "God has not an attribute which could take sides with the oppressor against the oppressed."

Not only in the Mosaic law, respecting service and labor, is there no principle or element analogous to that which constitutes American Slavery, *but in the bondage of the Hebrews in Egypt, even, there were no circumstances, no principles, no elements in common with it.*

Hard as was Pharaoh's heart, and bad soever as the legislative, judicial, and executive action of his government can be made out to be, there was in it scarce the slightest shade of cruelty and inhumanity, *compared* with the atrocities and barbarities of American slaveholding legislation, judicial and executive governmental action. And yet for what there was of injustice and cruelty *in the laws of Egypt*, God visited her with plagues and ultimate ruin.

I. Egyptian Servitude.

Let us glance briefly at a few characteristics of the bondage of the Hebrews in the land of Egypt, under the government of Pharaoh, as authenticated by the unerring pen of inspiration. In the Mosaic record the following points are made plain, —

First. *That the Hebrews, as a people, dwelt in a por-*

tion of Egypt specially allotted for their settlement. "And Joseph placed his father and his brethren, and gave them *a possession* in the land of Egypt, in the best of the land, in the land of Rameses, as Pharaoh had commanded." "And Israel dwelt in the land of Egypt, in the country of Goshen ; *and they had possessions therein, and grew and multiplied exceedingly.*" See Gen. xlvii. 5, 6, 11, 27.

This possession, let it be remembered, was given to the Hebrews, in the time of Joseph, *by the crown of Egypt,* when they numbered but seventy souls, and had been held by them up to the time of their departure from the land, a period of two hundred and fifteen years,* as appears from Exo. xii., 37 : "And the children of Israel *journeyed from Rameses,*" the place where Jacob at first settled on his coming into Egypt.

SECOND. The Hebrews not only dwelt in *a portion* of the land of Egypt, specially allotted to their possession, but it was *the best portion* of the land. Gen. xlvii. 6, 11. An obvious reason for the appropriation of the best portion of the land to the family of Jacob, was the sense

---

* In Exo. xii. 40, it is stated, " The sojourning of the children of Israel, who dwelt in Egypt, was *four hundred and thirty years.*" In Gen. xv. 13, it is told Abraham that his seed " *should be afflicted four hundred years.*" In Gal. iii. 17, Paul alludes to the promise made to Abraham as four hundred and thirty years before the giving of the law on Mount Sinai, which was the year of their deliverance from Egypt, just fifty days after their departure. The three passages, compared with some collateral ones, make the whole record plain. Thus, from the time God made the promise to Abraham of the land of Canaan, to the time of the departure of his seed from the land of Egypt, was four hundred and thirty years. From the time of Ishmael's mocking of Isaac, his promised seed, the period of reckoning the beginning of affliction, was four hundred years, while the actual sojourn of the twelve families or tribes of Jacob was only two hundred and fifteen years. The language of the record is worthy of special notice. It does not say that the *sojourning was all that time in Egypt,* but that the period of " the sojourning," or *unsettled state,* of Abraham and his seed, from the time of promise up to the period of deliverance, should be four hundred and thirty years.

of obligation to Joseph, for his instrumentality in saving
the land of Egypt from utter destruction by means of
the famine.

THIRD. Another feature of great importance to be considered, is the *peculiar tenure* by which this possession of
the land was held.

It has been remarked that the possession was granted
by the crown. The rightful possession of it, in perpetuity, was never questioned or denied by any of the successive reigning monarchs of the kingdom ; nor the attempt even alleged to have been made to dispossess
them of their estates.

To have a clear view of the whole matter, it should
be remembered, that during the continuance of the seven
years of famine, "Joseph gathered up all the money that
was found in the land of Egypt and in the land of
Canaan for the corn which they bought." That when
money failed, they gave their cattle for food — horses,
flocks, and herds ; *and, ultimately, all their lands,* so that
the land became Pharaoh's. Gen. xlvii. 13–20. But the
priests "sold not their lands," they being sustained by
"the portions which Pharaoh gave them." ver. 22.

The land given to the Hebrews was likewise not released to the crown. For "*Joseph nourished his father
and his brethren, and all his father's household, with bread,
according to their families.*" ver. 12. At the conclusion of
the famine, therefore, the land of Rameses, and the land
of the priests, were the only portions of the land of Egypt
which did not belong to Pharaoh.

After the famine, the land was appropriated by the
crown, for occupation and cultivation by the people, *as
tenants,* for which they were to pay to Pharaoh *one fifth
part* of the productions. ver. 26. But the lands of the
priests and the Hebrews did not come under the provis-

ions of this law. Their estates were held in fee simple, and the productions of the soil were, therefore, all at their own disposal.

Thus much for *the difference of tenure* by which the native Egyptians and the Hebrews held and occupied *their lands.*

With a clear apprehension of this relation to the government of Egypt, many other considerations and facts respecting the state of the Hebrews will be easily understood ; as, for example, —

FOURTH. They built, owned, and dwelt in their own houses — not in their *masters'* houses — for they *had* no masters, except *taskmasters* in the latter part of their sojourn in Egypt. Their family organizations were preserved intact, — their family relationships distinct. Read Exo. xii. 27. "It is the Lord's passover, who passed over *the houses of the children of Israel* in Egypt, when he smote the Egyptians, and delivered *our houses.*" See also vs. 22, 23, requiring the blood to be sprinkled on the lintel and side-posts of the door, lest the destroying angel should enter. There is not a particle of evidence that any individual of the Hebrews, male or female, lived with, or dwelt in any house that belonged to, an Egyptian. The circumstances of the Bible narrative all go to show that the reverse was true. For example (Exo. viii. 20–23), "Thus saith the Lord, Let my people go, that they may serve me. Else, if thou wilt not let my people go, behold, I will send swarms of flies upon thee, and upon thy servants, and upon thy people, and into *thy houses ; and the houses of the Egyptians* shall be full of swarms of flies, and *also the ground whereon they are.* And I will sever in that day *the land of Goshen, in which my people dwell,* that no swarms of flies shall be there ; to the end thou mayest know that I am the Lord in the midst of the earth. And I will put a division between my people and thy people." "And there came a grievous swarm of flies into the house of Pharaoh, and into *his servants' houses, and into all the* land of Egypt; *the land* was corrupted by reason of the swarms of flies."

None of the Hebrews were there. They were by them-selves — in their own land — in their own houses — in their respective family circles. Then Exo. ix. 3–12, respecting the plague of murrain upon the cattle, — "*God severed between the cattle of Israel and Egypt;*" — and the plague of boils upon man and upon beasts; and thus with all the successive plagues, — read the 7th, 8th, 9th, 10th, 11th, and 12th chapters of Exodus, particularly chapter 10, 22d and 23d verses, — "*all the children of Israel had light in their dwellings.*"

FIFTH. As the Hebrews were proprietors of the soil they tilled, of the habitations in which they lived, by guarantee of the Egyptian crown, so also they were al-lowed to manage all the affairs of their tribes and fami-lies and estates, according to their own pleasure, subject only to the general government and rule of the empire. Had their position being otherwise, it cannot easily be conceived how they would be able to preserve and keep correct genealogical records of their families and tribes back to the period of Abraham.

That they had their own internal governmental organ-izations, with appropriate officers, appears from Exo. v. 14, 15, 19, and vi. 14, where "*the officers of the children of Israel*" were beaten by *the taskmasters of Pharaoh;* and where a distinct recognition is made of "*the heads of their fathers' houses.*"

They had been permitted, and formerly without interrup-tion, to enjoy the right of assembling together peaceably, for the consideration of their affairs as a people, and continued to do it, even up to the period of their deliverance, though under oppressive governmental restrictions; as appears from Exo. iii. 16, where God commands Moses to " *gather the elders of Israel togethe*," and deliver the message he had specially addressed to them. The narrative contained in the twelfth chapter of Exodus, from the 3d to the 28th verse, goes to show their custom and habit of assembling by themselves at pleasure, as families and tribes, and observing religious ordinances and rites according to the convictions of their own consciences. The people assembled at the call of Moses, through the elders, and did as they were instructed. Exo. xii. 3, 21, 28.

SIXTH. From the considerations and facts preceding, it will be seen that the relations of the Hebrews to the government of Egypt were similar to the relations often subsisting between the nations of antiquity, of provinces, dependencies, or tributaries.

SEVENTH. This also affords a key to *the manner, kind, and extent of service* exacted of the Hebrews.

When Oriental governments employed their own legitimate subjects, or tributaries, in labor, it was then, as now, *in the form of a levy,* requiring the people to furnish a given quota. These were drafted off periodically, so that the same persons were not necessarily drawn away from their homes but for a limited period at any one time.

If the exactions were required in money, or other materials, for governmental support, the sums of money or provisions were specified, and periodically collected. See Josh. xvii. 13, and Judg. i. 28; 1 Kings ix. 21; 2 Kings xxiii. 33.

The particular service exacted, by the Egyptian government of the Hebrews, was " in mortar and in brick, and in all manner of service in the field." Exo. i. 14.

The direct *purpose* of this service, was the building *for the government* " *treasure cities.*" ver. 11. There is no indication or evidence that any individual subject or citizen of the government of Egypt, ever demanded, or was allowed the service of any Hebrew, without compensation, or against his will. There is no evidence that any *Hebrew female* was ever called into service by an Egyptian, except in the case of the mother of Moses, whose service, by the way, was *earnestly proffered, and generously paid for, by the daughter of the reigning monarch.* Exo. ii. 9.

The service to which the Hebrews were subjected was, *service to the government.* And the complaint against the government, and for which God visited them with plagues, was not for *demanding* service, but only as to the *manner* and *extent* of it. It was *right* that the Hebrews should do something for the support of the Egyptian government. The native Egyptians furnished their support of the crown *by rendering one fifth part of the productions of the soil.* But as the lands held by the Hebrews did not belong to the crown, exactions in this specific form could not reasonably be made. Therefore the exaction was made according to the pleasure of the king, *in the form of labor.* This was deemed politic for sundry reasons. Two prominent ones suggested were, *first*, to subdue and crush the spirit of the people ; *second*, to build cities to hold his vast and rapidly accumulating treasures of grain, from the fifth portion of the products of the soil cultivated by his native subjects.

Now, had this exaction of labor from the Hebrews not been more than an equivalent for one fifth portion of the productions of the soil, they would not have had any special reason to complain, any more, at farthest, than had the native Egyptians against their own government. But this was not the case. The Hebrews were made

*not only to serve, but " to serve with rigor." Unreasonable
and cruel exactions were made of them. " Their lives were
made bitter with hard bondage."*

But it should not be supposed that the whole people
were subjected, *personally and individually*, to active
service in the fields of the crown, or in making brick and
mortar for Pharaoh's treasure cities. The circumstances
narrated in the Mosaic record show to the contrary, and
show that a large portion of the people were habitually
at their homes, and in the cultivation of their own lands,
and in the care of their own flocks and herds, or engaged
in other business or industrial employments.

But by exactions made upon them of service and labor,
beyond what justice and equity would allow, *the Hebrews, as a people, were afflicted and oppressed.*

That many of the people had liberty and opportunity
to devote themselves to the cultivation of science and the
arts, — of music, metallurgy, engraving, embroidery, &c.,
— will be evident on a careful perusal of chapters 25, 26,
27, 28, 35, 36, of the book of Exodus.

Such are some of the considerations and facts exhibit-
ing the prominent characteristics of the system of service
and labor to which the Hebrews were subjected by the
government of Egypt.

In the bondage of the Hebrews in Egypt, they had
their own form of civil polity, as respected themselves,
with officers of their own choice ; — *a home government,* —
subject, like colonial dependencies of ancient and modern
days, to the government of the crown. They had a sec-
tion of country to themselves, lived in communities by
themselves, built and lived in their own houses, on their
own lands ; raised, tended, and owned " a multitude of
flocks and herds," a large portion of the nation having
time not only to care properly for their lands, and flocks,

and herds, but to devote to science and the arts, with freedom, also, to inculcate and attend to the instructions of their religion, and to worship the God of their fathers. There was no dispersion of the individuals or families of the Hebrews among the families of Egypt. No ownership, no pretence or claim to ownership, by any Egyptian, king or subject, of any individual of all the Hebrew tribes.

In short, in the oppressions of the Hebrews by the Egyptian government, there was not one principle, element, or provision of law, which involved the characteristic, elemental principle of every slave code of the American slave States. In no instance or respect was there recognized the principle or element of *the chattellization of humanity* — the principle of property in man — never a legislative, judicial and executive, legal and governmental adjudging the Hebrews, or any one of them, " as goods and chattels personal, in the hands of their masters and possessors, to all intents, constructions, and purposes whatsoever."

Need we pause to compare the governmental administration of Pharaoh, in regard to the service and labor of the Hebrews, with the governmental provisions of law, and administration of the slaveholding States, regarding the people they hold in bondage?

Yet how can we forbear to stop a moment, to inquire whether or not, they who are called " servants," at the South, have, out of paternal kindness, governmentally given and appropriated to them, as a possession, an extensive tract of country, *for their exclusive occupation —* yea, even " *the best of the land*"? Have they, whom the South calls servants, by provisions of law, the liberty and right to have and to hold, or dispose of at pleasure, the products of their soil and of their labor? — to have and to hold "very much cattle," and "a multitude of flocks"? Have their servants the liberty and privilege of adopting and enjoying their own civil polity, pertaining to their own internal affairs?—their own home government, with officers of their own choice?—the liberty and opportunity of education in science and religion? Are all the females held in bondage at the South, exempt from all exactions of labor, by their masters, and by the strong arm of law protected from insolence and outrage?

But why pursue these inquiries? Why urge these contrasts further?

The Egyptian system of service and labor, bad soever as it may be made to appear, either in principle or application, was benevolence, justice, and mercy embodied, *compared* with the system of American Slavery, by which a man is robbed of everything—even his every attribute of humanity!

To whatever other hardships the Hebrews were subjected, they testify to the fact, that they were plentifully supplied with food. "We sat by the flesh-pots, and did eat bread to the full." Exo. xvi. 3. "We did eat fish freely; the cucumbers, and the melons, and the leeks, and the onions, and the garlic." Numb. xi. 5.

Whatever may be said of the servitude to which the Hebrews were subjected in Egypt, there was the entire absence of those features of cruelty and barbarism, which characterize the American slave codes,—the abrogation of marriage and the family relation—the incapacity of the slave to acquire and hold property—the denial of all civil and political rights—the denial of all facilities and means of education; and other items of cruelty and oppression too numerous and barbarous to be recited here in detail.

3

And yet, for *the oppressions of Egypt*, God smote her with plagues, and trampled upon her as the mire of the street, till her pride and power had passed away.

If God is no respecter of *nations*, what has not this land reason to anticipate at the hands of an avenging God?

But, it should be remembered, the severe oppression of the Hebrews, did not continue during the whole period of their sojourn in the land of Egypt.

In the days, and for the sake, of Joseph, their deliverer and savior, and for some time thereafter, the government of Egypt dealt *kindly*, even *paternally*, *patronizingly* and *partially* toward them. This policy continued until, under the blessing of God, the Hebrews had "increased abundantly, and multiplied and waxed exceeding mighty." Exo. i. 7, 9.

The jealousy of the reigning monarch becoming excited by their prosperity, as a people, he resorted to a policy which involved *oppression*, in order, as he thought needful, to preserve the integrity and safety of his kingdom.

But failing to crush the spirit and check the growth of the people by the rigor of the means thus far employed, and his fears becoming still more strongly excited by a prophetical annunciation, that one was to be born to the Hebrews, who was to subvert his throne, and be their deliverer, he issued a special proclamation, requiring all the male children, born for a certain period from that time, to be put to death — thinking, by this means, to prevent the fulfilment of the prophetical prediction.

This act of cruelty and murder, it is believed, did not originate in any delight of Pharaoh to inflict or witness suffering and distress, *but in his fears of the subversion of his kingdom.* He adopted it, very likely, as a measure of *necessity*, in accordance with the sentiment, "Self-preservation is the first law of nature."

At a later period in Jewish history, *through a similar fear*, King Herod commanded the destruction of the male children of Bethlehem and its coasts. Matt. ii.

Though there was, in the acts of the government before this, sufficient to provoke the wrath of God, yet this edict to destroy the children, was the climax of governmental wickedness — "the filling up of its measure of iniquity" — the filling up of the cup of sorrow, distress, and anguish of the Hebrew commonwealth. "*They cried unto the Lord!*" And He heard their cry, and came down to deliver and save them.

But this measure of cruelty and wickedness — the destruction of the male Hebrew children — was not the *ordinary*, or *usual policy* of the Egyptian government. It was an *extra-ordinary measure*, adopted under *extraordinary circumstances*, and should, therefore, be considered and judged of by itself, in the light of the peculiar circumstances under which it was adopted, and not as characteristic of the ordinary government policy.

But even in this culmination of wickedness and barbarism, Pharaoh came very far short of reaching that climax of iniquity in governmental administration, to which the authors and supporters of American Slavery have attained.

II. The Mosaic System of Service and Labor.

We come now to the consideration of the Patriarchal system of service, as established and supported by the Mosaic law.

By a brief survey of this law, I think it will be shown, at one and the same time, and by the same means, that it not only *lacks* every *principle and element of injustice* complained of against Egypt, but that there is contained in it not one provision or element *like*, or in fellowship *with*, American Slavery.

The provisions of the Mosaic law were all founded in benevolence toward the servant, as well as justice toward the master. They were all founded on the law of *love*.

That there is no resemblance between the two systems, *either in principles or provisions*, a few brief statements will clearly show.

I. Any *one* of several distinct provisions of the Mosaic law, if applied to American Slavery, would sweep away *the whole foundation and superstructure* of the American slave code.

I will mention the following as a few examples : —

1. Deut. xxiii. 15, 16. "Thou shalt not deliver unto his master the servant which *is escaped* from his master unto thee. He shall dwell with thee, even among you in that place which he shall choose, in one of thy gates where it liketh him best ; thou shalt not oppress him."

Apply *this one provision* to the slaves of the South, and what becomes of "the peculiar institution"? Observe, *the law is imperative*, "Thou shalt not deliver unto the master the servant that is escaped unto thee." No matter for what reason he left, he shall not be delivered up.

2. In juxtaposition with the foregoing, read another provision of this law, where the time of service expires, and the servant desires to remain with his employer — Exo. xxi. 2–6. The master has no power or right to refuse his stay, but is obliged to continue him in his service, on terms similar to those on which the relation was entered.

Both provisions go to show, that the advantage, if any, was on the side of the servant. The servant could go when and where he pleased; but the master could not send him away, after a specified term of service, if the servant was disposed to continue.

3. Exod. xxi. 26, 27. "If a man smite the eye of his servant, or the eye of his maid, that it perish, he shall let him go free for his eye's sake. And if he smite out his man-servant's tooth, or his maid-servant's tooth, he shall let him go free for his tooth's sake." And thus for any other bodily injury.

Let this principle be incorporated into the American slave code, and how many of the four millions of slaves would remain this day in bondage?

4. *Under the Mosaic law there could be no compulsory service or labor.* No individual, Hebrew or stranger, man or woman, worked for another, *except from choice.*

This is made clear from the passage already quoted, Deut. xxiii. 15, 16: "Thou shalt not deliver unto his master the servant which is escaped," &c. To deliver him up would recognize the right of the master to hold him. This right is denied. The servant's fleeing from his master, shows his choice, proclaims his master's oppressive or unkind treatment, and furnishes his claim to legal protection.

This regulation has no restriction or qualification. It relates to servants taken from the Hebrews and the Gentiles alike. There was one law for both. And it mattered not whether the servant escaped from a Hebrew, from a stranger sojourning among the Hebrews, or from one of another nation, he was entitled to, and received protection, just as our government extends protection to exiles of other lands, who flee to our shores for refuge.

With this provision of the Mosaic law, *there could be*

3 *

no compulsory labor. "Thou shalt not deliver him up," under any pretext whatsoever. "He shall dwell in the place which he shall choose." "*Thou shalt not oppress him,*" implying that *the restraint of his own choice,* as to *the place and conditions of his service, or of his residence,* IS OPPRESSION.

There was never a servant held, *under the Mosaic law,* who was not as free in choice, respecting the place and conditions of service and residence, as any man in New England.

5. Another consideration of great importance, shedding light upon the former positions, as well as constituting, in itself, an important feature in the provisions of the Mosaic law, respecting service and labor, is, that *all servants received pay for their own work.* They never consented or contracted to work without pay. If pay was withheld, in any instance, it was in palpable violation of law, and by the explicit declaration of Jehovah, greatly provocative of his wrath.

A single passage in Jeremiah, xxii. 13, will show how that prophet regarded the provisions of this law, respecting service and labor : " Wo unto him that buildeth his house by unrighteousness and his chambers by wrong; that useth his neighbor's service *without wages,* and giveth *him* not for his work."

This was a judgment pronounced under the Mosaic law of service. The Prophet recognized — knew no other.

The Apostle James, under the New Testament Dispensation, gives utterance to like views : " Behold, *the hire of the laborers,* who have reaped down your fields, which is of you kept back, *by fraud, crieth,* and the cries of them which have reaped, are reached unto the ears of the Lord of Sabaoth," chap. v. 4 ; referring, evidently, to the words of Moses in the law : "If thou shalt afflict them, *in any wise*, and they cry at all unto me, I will hear their cry, and my wrath shall wax hot. I will kill your children with the sword," &c. Exo. xxii. 23, 24. The numerous allusions to this subject in the Scriptures, all unite to show, that, *under the Mosaic law*, *no servant ever wrought without wages.* If pecuniary compensation was ever withheld, it was withheld *by fraud.*

6. It is worthy, also, of distinct remark, that the wages required by the law to be paid for labor, were to be paid *to the servant, by his employer — not to another man* : " and giveth *him* not for *his* work."

There is nothing here of the slaveholding policy and arrangement, of *masters* getting pay for their servants' work.

7. As it has been shown that a servant was *at liberty* to leave his master, if he saw good cause, so it is worthy of distinct remark, that the master had no control over his servant *to sell his services to another man, much less to sell the man himself.*

On this point there is, doubtless, much vagueness of conception and great misapprehension.' These arise, in part, from the misconception of terms employed in the record of transactions of those ancient days, such as the terms " bought with money," " sold," &c.

There are those who take for granted that whatever is said to be " bought with money," or " sold for money," *must be* money, or subject to the condition and attributes of money, as an article of traffic or exchange. They take this for granted, not only *without proof*, but *in face of evidence* to the contrary. It is very convenient for them to do so, as it saves them the labor of investigation and of solid argument.

A few examples for illustration. The children of

Israel were required to " redeem," or *purchase* their first born from under the obligations of the priesthood, by the payment of a sum of money. Numb. xviii. 15, 16; Exo. xxxiv. 20.   By this process of procuring a release from certain obligations by a certain sum of money, were all the first born of Israel converted into goods and chattels?

Boaz " *purchased* Ruth the Moabitess to be his wife." Ruth iv. 10.   Was she, therefore, adjudged and held as property — as goods and chattels personal?

Jacob *bought* his two wives at a cost of seven years' service for each. Gen. xxix. 20–30.   David purchased Michal, the daughter of King Saul (1 Sam. xviii. 25), and Othniel purchased the daughter of Caleb (Judges i. 12, 13), by performing perilous services for the benefit of their fathers-in-law.   The prophet Hosea "bought" his wife, paying for her partly in money and partly in grain, — " fifteen pieces of silver and a homer and a half of barley." Hos. iii. 2.

The purchase of wives with money or by service was the general practice.   The language of the passage above referred to (1 Sam. xviii. 25), is illustrative of this fact. " The king desireth not any *dowry*, but an hundred foreskins of the Philistines," implying that " dowry," in some form, was always expected.

When Shechem interceded for Dinah, the daughter of Jacob, to become his wife, he said (Gen. xxxiv. 11, 12), " Let me find grace in your eyes, and what ye shall say unto me I will give.   Ask me never so much dowry and gift, and I will give according as ye shall say unto me; but give me the damsel to wife."   See also Gen. xxiv. 53 ; 2 Sam. iii. 14.

The Mosaic law provides for this very thing — the sale or gift of daughters, for dowry, *to become wives, — not slaves* — not as merchandise — subject to be re-sold, as articles of traffic. Deut. xxii. 28, 29.

The *idea* or *principle of chattelism*, in which American Slavery, according to its own codes, *consists*, involves the condition or quality of *transfer* — *of traffic* — *of sale*. But this idea, or principle, is nowhere incorporated or recognized, in the provisions of the Mosaic law, respecting any human being, nor in the practice of the Patriarchs antecedently to the giving of that law on Sinai.

Let us look at the case of "Father Abraham," to whose position, toward his servants, reference is so often made, in support of Slavery.

The first mention we have of Abraham, *in connection with servants*, is in the thirteenth chapter of Genesis, subsequent to his sojourn in Egypt during a period of famine in the land of Canaan. In the connection it is stated that "*Abraham was very rich in cattle, in silver, and in gold;*" also, that "there was a strife between the herdmen of Abraham's cattle and the herdmen of Lot's cattle." No mention is made, before this, of herdmen, either as belonging to Abraham or Lot. But many they must unquestionably have had, as it is distinctly stated "that their substance was great, so that they could not dwell together." Still we have no clew to the *number* of servants which either of them had. But further along in the history (chap. xiv.) we have the statement that Abraham "*armed his trained servants, born in his house, three hundred and eighteen.*" The next characteristic mentioned of these servants, is contained in chap. xiv. 24, where Abraham speaks of them to the king of Sodom as "*young men.*"

These "young men" are not inventoried among Abraham's "goods and chattels," as constituting any part of his riches; though the mention of their *number*

is a very clear indication of the extent of his possessions.
If they had been regarded and held by Abraham *as property*, they would doubtless have been inventoried, in accordance with the custom of our Southern Patriarchs of
Slavery. And this inventory of " goods and chattels "
would have amounted to quite a little figure. According
to the usual basis of reckoning, the *three hundred and
eighteen servants, born in his house, all young men, trained
and able to go forth to war*, would indicate in his employ
servants of all classes, not less than two or three thousand. These, at the average estimate of reckoning among
our Southern Patriarchs, would make an item in his inventory of over a million of dollars. But they are not
thus inventoried or regarded.

That the servants of Abraham were all *voluntary* in
their service, is evident from numerous considerations,
of which one alone will suffice — *the impossibility of keeping them against their wills.* Abraham was no king —
had no empire — no constitution and form of civil government — no political schemes of ambition to achieve.
He was simply a wealthy shepherd — had an immense
property in flocks and herds, as well as in silver and gold.
But he was not the proprietor of the soil he occupied
with his flocks. He was a citizen and subject of the
kings, in whose countries he sought and found pasturage
for his flocks. Under such circumstances, if his servants
had been disposed to leave him, it was impossible for him
to prevent it. They could also, at any time, have combined together to destroy him and his, with no earthly
power to hinder. Besides, the neighboring tribes, instead
of helping him to *keep* his servants, would have been
ready, on every favorable opportunity, to help them
away.

But, it is asked, what is the meaning and purport of

the expression in the record (Gen. xvii. 12, 13) —
" *bought with money* " ?

" Of *whom* did he buy them? " That is the question
to be answered. Do you affirm that he bought them of
third parties? That is begging the question to be proved.
*And I challenge the record of an intimation, or of an in-
stance, of the sale of a servant, by anybody but himself
— of a single case, under the Patriarchal or the Mosaic
systems,* in which *a master sold his* servant.

I will, however, admit and name an instance in which
the Patriarchs made a very conspicuous figure in the sale
of a fellow-being. It was not, however, one in the relation of a *servant*. It is recorded in Gen. xxxvii. 28, and
referred to by Stephen (Acts vii. 9), in these words:
"And the Patriarchs, moved with envy, sold Joseph
into Egypt." The *price* they received for him, was
twenty pieces of silver — about one third less than Judas
Iscariot obtained for a like betrayal of his Lord and
Master.

If these examples are of any service and value to the
advocates of chattelism, they are welcome to all the aid
and comfort of such precedents. But in neither of these
cases was there the understanding or pretence of any
property title conveyed. It was palpably plain, and understood by all parties, that the bargain and sale involved
no pretence to claim of ownership, as goods and chattels.
Yet had the Mosaic law been in force, when Joseph's
brethren sold him into Egypt, every one of them con-
senting to the crime, would have been put to death, according to Exo. xxi. 6: " He that stealeth a man and
selleth him, or if he be found in his hand, he shall surely
be put to death."

To " steal," is to take and appropriate to one's use,
without consent, what belongs to another. " Stealeth

a man" — of or from whom shall he be stolen? — *from his master?* He is *a man* — belongs, under God, *to himself* — to steal HIM, is to rob him of his self-control — to appropriate him to another's use by force or constraint.

To do this, under the Mosaic law, was a capital crime — was an infraction of a fundamental principle of that law, and the common judgment of mankind — as set forth in the Declaration of Independence by our fathers.

Is it a self-evident truth, that some other party has a proprietary right in a man, rather than himself? — That it is to be *presumed* that a man belongs to somebody besides himself?

I have before alluded to the case where *daughters were sold by their fathers*, but, in all cases, *to become wives.* The instances of this kind on record are numerous. *If servants were bought of third persons*, where is the intimation or record of the fact?

In Levit. xxv. 47, we have the record, *"If thy brother . . . sell himself."* In the 39th verse of the same chapter, the same word and the same form of the word, which is rendered above, *" sell himself,"* is rendered *" be sold;"* and in Deut. xxviii. 68, in like manner, where, both for the true grammatical construction of the record, as well as for the true import of the language, it should be rendered, *" ye shall offer yourselves for sale . . . and no man shall buy you."* Whereas, by the current rendering, the statement in the record is self-contradictory — ye shall *be* sold . . . and *no man shall buy you."*

There are numerous passages of Scripture which afford a key to the *usage of language* on this point, as for example, Rom. vi. 16 : *"Know ye not that to whom ye yield yourselves servants to obey*, his servants ye are to whom ye obey."

The force of this figure is lost, on the supposition that

the relation of servants to masters was *compulsory*. The same is true of John viii. 34 : " Whosoever committeth sin *is the servant of sin.*" It is a voluntary relation. 1 Kings xxi. 25 : " There was none like unto Ahab, which *did sell himself*, to work wickedness," &c. Isa. lii. 3 : " Ye have *sold yourselves for nought,*" &c. Also, l. 1 ; 2 Kings xvii. 17.

From the record in Gen. xlvii. 18–26, it appears that Joseph made a large purchase of servants. But of whom did he buy them? The people of Egypt came to him with the entreaty, " *Buy us and our land, for bread.*" And he did buy all their land for Pharaoh, and the land became Pharaoh's. So Joseph says, also, " I have bought *you* this day," &c. The *land* he bought *first* of the Egyptians, — " for the Egyptians sold every man his field." Of whom did he buy *them ?* Each one *of himself.* But being bought, how were *they* regarded and treated? *Like goods and chattels?* Is there a word of intimation to that effect?

But the record of this transaction by Joseph, while ruler of Egypt, I have not referred to as proving anything in reference to the provisions of the Mosaic law in regard to servants, as they transpired antecedently to the giving of the law, and had no connection with it ; but simply to show the *usage* of language in regard to such transactions.

But if the objector insists that the language " bought with money," or " sold," involves the principle of chattelism, let him remember that by such interpretation he makes goods and chattels of all the wives of the patriarchs themselves, and of all the Jewish commonwealth.

But in the case of Abraham, even if it could be proved that he bought his servants of a *third party*, it does not prove that he regarded or held them as goods and chat-

4

tels ; or even if he did, that the principles and provisions
of the Mosaic law would sanction such a position.

But let us look a step farther into the provisions of
the Mosaic law regarding servants.

1. *Servants are placed on a level with their masters' in
all their civil and religious rights.* Levit. xxiv. 22 :
" Ye shall have one manner of law, as well for the
stranger as for one of your own country." Deut. i. 16,
17 : " I charged your judges at that time, saying, Hear
the causes between your brethren, and judge righteously
between every man and his brother, and the stranger
that is with him. Ye shall not respect persons in
judgment," &c. See also Numb. ix. 1, 4, and xv. 15,
16, 29.

2. *Servants were admitted into covenant with God on
the same terms with their masters.* Deut. xxix. 10–13 .
" Ye stand this day, all of you, before the Lord thy God ;
your captains of your tribes, your elders, and your officers ; with all the men of Israel, your little ones, your
wives, and *thy stranger* that is in thy camp, from the
hewer of thy wood unto the drawer of thy water, that
thou shouldest enter into covenant with the Lord thy
God," &c.

3. Servants were not only *invited*, but *required* to be
present at all the national and family festivals, with the
households to whom they were attached. Deut. xii. 10
–12 : " Ye shall rejoice before the Lord your God, ye,
and your sons, and your daughters, and your *men servants
and your maid servants*, and the Levite that is within
your gates ; " and in Deut. xvi. 9–12, there is added,
" *and the stranger that is within thy gates*," &c.

4. Servants were to be *allowed, and required to attend
upon, the same means of religious instruction with their
masters.* Deut. xxxi. 12 : " Gather the people together

men, and women, and children, and *thy stranger that is
within thy gates, that they may hear, and that they may
learn*, and fear the Lord your God, and do all the words
of this law." See Josh. viii. 33-35; 2 Chron. xvii.
8, 9.

To form some proper estimate of the importance and
value of these provisions of the law to the servant, their
practical operation should be considered.

Besides the *direct advantages* already indicated, it is
well to understand from what they were exonerated and
released.

5. The law provides for those servants whose term of
service extends over seven years, *every seventh year* exemption from work. Then in attendance on the three
annual festivals — the feast of the Passover, the feast of
Pentecost, and the feast of Tabernacles, each for one
week or more — then the feasts of New Moons, the feasts
of Trumpets, and others, involving a release from active
service, in the aggregate, of about one hundred and
eighty or more days, or of nearly or fully one half of
every year.

6. It is also easy to see, that in the intimate religious
fellowships, so frequent, so almost constant, so familiar,
that strong mutual affection and attachment would be
likely to result.

This was the design of the Lawgiver in this arrangement, and in accordance with his repeatedly expressed
injunctions; as Levit. xix. 34: " *The stranger* that
dwelleth with you shall be unto you as one born among
you, and *thou shalt love him as thyself*." Deut. x. 17–19:
"For the Lord thy God . . . *loveth the stranger*, in
giving him food and raiment, *love ye therefore the
stranger*." See Exo. xxii. 21, and xxiii. 9; Levit. xxv.
35, 36.

7. With all the preceding considerations in view, it will be no marvel to find permanent social, family relationships established. This was of very frequent occurrence. To this Solomon alludes in his Proverbs, xxix. 21 : " He that delicately bringeth up his servant, from a child, shall have him become his son at the length." An instance of this is particularly recorded in 1 Chron. ii. 34, 35.

8. Intimately connected with the preceding, is the privilege of *heirship*. To this allusion is made in Prov. xvii. 2 : " A wise *servant* shall have rule over a son that causeth shame, *and shall have part of the inheritance among the brethren.*" Also, in Mark xii. 7 : " This is the *heir ;* come, let us kill *him, and the inheritance shall be ours.*" This conclusion was based on the provisions of the law, that where there was the lack of posterity, the servant or servants became sole heirs to the estate.

Abraham alludes to this in Gen. xv. 2, 3 : " Behold, to me thou hast given no seed, and lo, one born in my house is mine heir ; " alluding to Eliezer of Damascus, his steward.

The foregoing and numerous other considerations go to show, that the relationship of " *bought servants,*" was one, not only involving equity, justice, equality before the law, compensation for services rendered, equality in the enjoyment of religious privileges and instructions, but of kind and tender affection, like that of parents towards their children. The supervision and control of their masters, when in accordance with the divine requisitions, were those of the father over his own offspring. Thus thought Paul, who may be presumed to have had some correct understanding of the Mosaic law. Gal. iv. 1, 2 : " Now I say, that the heir, so long as he is a child, *differeth nothing from a servant,* though he be Lord of all," &c.

Notwithstanding, however, the clearness with which the sacred record states all the points considered, there are those who profess to find portions of the record which clearly allow and maintain the principle of property in man. Among the expressions relied on to maintain this position, are such as occur in Levit. xxv. 44–46 : " Thy *bondmen* shall be of the heathen ; . . . of them shall ye buy :" " they shall be your possession" "and your bondmen forever."

After what has been said, clearly establishing the position, relations, and condition of servants, a few words of explanation would seem to be all that is necessary to rescue such expressions from an interpretation subversive of all the established principles and provisions of the law.

The word rendered *bondmen* here, is the same elsewhere uniformly rendered *servants.* In Isa. xlii. 1, the same word is applied to Christ : " Behold my servant, whom I uphold ; " and lii. 13 : " Behold my servant shall deal prudently," &c. In 1 Kings xii. 7, it is applied alike to the king and his subjects : " If *thou* wilt be *a servant* (Ebed) unto this people this day, . . . then *they* will be *thy servants* forever."

The word is applied *to all persons doing service to others,* without regard to their position, place, or manner of service — to rulers, prophets, priests, and people. No other word was needful to express any manner of service sanctioned or recognized by the provisions of the Mosaic law, or the usages of the patriarchs. Had a relation existed, analogous to that of *a slave,* there would have been *some word representing it in distinction from any other*

4 *

relation. In our own language, the word SLAVE is used to represent a state and condition which no other one word can express; and is used, because *the thing exists which it is designed to represent.* The thing did NOT EXIST under the Mosaic law, and therefore no word is found to indicate it.

After what has been said respecting such terms as *bought, sold,* &c., it is needful, concerning the word " *buy,*" only to add, the suggestion, that it implies *a prohibition against taking men or women, as servants, by force, or taking them without pay,* as in subsequent history they were cursed repeatedly for doing. A Hebrew was not to receive even a *heathen* into his family and service, without the consideration of a contract of payment.

The other portions of this passage, " *Ye shall take them as an inheritance for your children,*" and " *they shall be your bondmen forever,*" relate to the permanency of the defined arrangement.

To interpret the passage as proof that *individual servants* were doomed to continue in that relation *during their lifetime,* and that their children after them were doomed to the same relation, would be to annul numerous specific provisions of the law.

The law was peremptory in commanding, that every fiftieth year — the year of Jubilee — *every servant should be set free.* No matter whether the servant had been in that relation four years or forty, *when the year of Jubilee came he was to be set at liberty. No bonds could hold over and beyond that time,* either in regard to service or the conveyance (with exceptions) of real estate. Read Levit. xxv. 8–34.

The language of the passage under consideration (xxv. 44–46) is designed to apply to *national* and not *individual* relations, — to prescribe *the source* from which they should obtain their servants, viz., *from the families of strangers*, and not from the Israelites. This should be their source of supply, throughout their generations — " forever " — a permanent arrangement.

As to the terms "possession" and "inheritance," as indicating any *property consideration* in the case of servants, it will suffice to advert to the numerous passages where such phraseology occurs. When Moses prays in behalf of Israel (Exo. xxxiv. 9), " Take *us* for thine *inheritance*," does he ask God to receive and take them as goods and chattels, or real estate?

Ezek. xliv. 28 : " I am thine *inheritance;* " Ps. xciv. 14 : " Neither will he forsake his *inheritance;* " — does God intend to represent himself and his people as goods and chattels — marketable commodities? We speak of the institutions of our own civil government, and of our religious privileges, as an *inheritance* left us by our fathers, — do we understand it in the light of *mere property* — as what is subject to the laws of traffic — of bargain and sale?

" But there is another provision and expression in the Mosaic law which cannot be explained away from its explicit declaration. It means just what it says." Exo. xxi. 20, 21 : " *For he is his money.*" " *There is no getting away from that.*" So says the defender of Slavery.

" This means just what it says " ! What wonderful sticklers for *literal interpretations !*

The words in the original are *kaspo-hu*, and would be more precisely rendered " his *silver* is he." In the language of another, " This principle of interpretation is the philosopher's stone ! Its miraculous touch transmutes five feet eight inches of flesh and bones into *solid silver.*"

Will the defenders of Slavery, who insist on this prin-

ciple of interpretation, in this particular case, abide by it
in similar cases? For example: "This *is* my body,"
"This *is* my blood." Matt. xxvi. 26, 28. "I am *the
bread which came down from heaven.*" John vi. 32, 33, 41,
and 53. "Except ye eat the flesh of the Son of man
and drink his blood, ye have no life in you;" and a
thousand others, both in the Old Testament and the
New.

But let us look at the passage in which the expression
occurs, and the connection in which it stands (Exo. xxi.
20, 21): "If a man smite his servant or his maid with
a rod, and he die under his hand, he shall surely be punished. Notwithstanding, if he continue a day or two,
he shall not be punished, for he is his money."

The whole passage is often quoted to prove that Hebrew masters, under the Mosaic law, not only had the
right to punish their servants *severely*, and at *their will*,
but that *they might whip them into* an *inch of their lives*,
and *be liable to no penalties!* If the servant *should die
under the master's hand, while he was whipping him*, he
should be *punished;* but if he did not go so far in whipping him, but that *he lived a day or two*, then no account
was to be made of it — no penalty was attached to the
transaction!

Such an interpretation of the genius and provisions of
the Mosaic law, I have no hesitancy in pronouncing *an
outrageous libel on the Divine Lawgiver* — involving him,
not only in outrageously *unrighteous and cruel, but ridicu-
lously inconsistent and contradictory, legislation.*

It has already been made plain, that *every man*, Hebrew or stranger, in regard to the protection of person
and property, stood on the same ground before the law
— that, in the case of a servant, if he saw good reason
to leave his master, he had the right to do so at his

pleasure — and that the government should protect him
against all attempts of his master to bring him back.
"*Thou shalt not deliver him up.*"

We have seen, also, that *if a man smite out his servant's tooth, even though it be by accident,* " he shall let him
go free for his tooth's sake." *And not that alone* — for
there is another provision of law applicable to this as
every other case — the *master, in addition,* should have
his own tooth smitten out. This was to be done *judicially*
— by action of the government, as a forfeiture to the
government for cruel and improper conduct, in violation
of law. The exemption of the servant from further service,
was *his* compensation, in part, for the loss of his tooth.
For any *nameless* unkind treatment, which made it un-
pleasant and painful or irksome for the servant to dwell
with his master, he might leave him, and his master's
interest in his services be sacrificed and lost.

And now, forsooth, we have an interpretation of a law
or statute, by which *a man may whip his servant to death*
(so that he dies in a day or two), and *escape without
any punishment at all ! !* " No, but he *is* punished *in
the loss of his servant's labor.*"

Then the punishment for a few nameless unkindnesses,
or the accidental knocking out of a tooth, by a passionate
stroke, is punished as severely as *the whipping him to
death ! ! Is that the Divine legislation ?* Do such *absurdities* obtain in the Mosaic law? *Never !* What is the
object of the statutory provision now under consideration?
Is it *to define how murder shall be punished ?* No. If a
man smites a servant, so that he dies under his hand,
this statute does not say what shall be done with the master. It only says, " *he shall be punished.*" *How* he shall
be punished is provided for elsewhere. If the servant
smitten does not die under his hand, but *lives a day or*

two, the master, it is here provided, "*shall not be pun-ished*," according to the current rendering. The Hebrew word, *Nakam*, it is said, occurs thirty-five times in the Old Testament, and in every instance, *except here*, is translated "*avenge*," or "*to take vengeance*," or "to re-venge."

With a like rendering here, the passage would read (the pronoun IT being used for HE), "IT (the death) *shall surely be avenged*," or "*by avenging it shall be avenged*,"— a term usually employed to indicate the pun-ishment for murder. In the latter of the two verses, in-stead of "he shall not be punished," it should read, "IT *shall not be avenged*." That is to say, the crime, in the first instance, shall be considered *murder*, and shall be *punished* as murder. In the latter case the crime shall not be *construed* as murder; the circumstances of the case favoring the conclusion that there was *no intention* to kill — that there was no *malice a-fore-thought* — and shall therefore be treated according to other requisitions of the law in such case provided. The crime would be *man-slaughter*, and not murder. The circumstances of the case, as here given, suppose:

1. That the man smitten was a *servant*.

2. Therefore, that the master had a pecuniary interest in his life, which it would be for his advantage to protect.

3. That *the instrument used was not a death weapon*, but simply *a rod* or switch.

4. That with *this* instrument he does not continue to beat him *till he dies*, as he would be *likely to do*, if he had previously intended to kill him.

These considerations taken together, shall be construed into *prima facie* evidence that it was not the master's in-tent to kill. If *other* evidence existed of such *intent, this circumstantial evidence* was overruled and set aside, and

the crime adjudged and treated as murder, and the provision for its punishment *was unmistakable.* Numb. xxxv.
30, 31 ; Levit. xxiv. 17. " Whoso *killeth* any person,
the murderer shall be surely put to death." " Moreover
ye shall take no satisfaction for the life of a murderer,
which is guilty of death ; but he shall be surely put to
death." Read also vs. 32, 33.

These considerations go to show, clearly, that the provisions of the law in this passage are *explanatory*, or *constructive.* The *object*, evidently, to settle, in. circumstantial cases, what shall be construed as murder, and what
otherwise. And to force a constructive statute, *directly*
intended to distinguish between murder and manslaugh-
ter, into a statute converting humanity into property,
simply because the pecuniary interest of a master in his
servant's life, shall be construed in his favor, in case of
trial for murder, exhibits a disposition to favor oppression and despotism not to be expected from the professed
friends of liberty and justice.

Before dismissing this case of the man who dies " in
a day or two," and of his master, it may be well to advert to some provisions made in the law for such cases.

We have already shown that in *this* case, the master is
not to be adjudged *a murderer* and his crime " *avenged.*"
We have already seen that, in case the master smites out
the eye or tooth of his servant, the servant is to go free
for his tooth's sake ; and, *besides and beyond* all forfeiture
to the servant, he is to be taken in hand by the officers
of law, and made an example before the people — *he is
to lose his own tooth. The same principle of law is applicable in all cases.*

Levit. xxiv. 18 : " He that killeth a beast (of his neighbor's) shall make it good, beast for beast." Ver. 19 : "And
if a man cause a blemish in his neighbor, *as he hath*

*done, so shall it be done unto him." "*Breach for breach,
eye for eye, tooth for tooth ; as he has caused a blemish
in a man, so shall it be done to him again." And Deut.
xix. 19, in reference to a *contemplated* injury to a man by
false testimony, " *Then shall ye do unto him as he had
thought to have done unto his brother ;* so shalt thou put
the evil away from among you." "And thine eye shall
not pity ; but life shall go for life, eye for eye, tooth for
tooth, hand for hand, and foot for foot."

The *end* of this administrative justice is declared to
be, " That those which remain shall hear and fear, and
shall henceforth commit no more any such evil among
you." 20.

Now, with all these examples and statutory provisions
before us, are we to be wheedled into the belief that a master, under the Mosaic law, who could not even use insult-
ing language toward his servant without losing all claim to
his services, — could not smite out his tooth or eye, without losing his services, besides himself losing a corresponding tooth, or eye,— could not inflict *any blemish,*
mutilate any limb, without losing his own through judicial proceedings, — I say, are we to suppose that when
he whips his servant so that he dies after a few days,
all that he is subjected to *is merely the loss of his property,*
in the death of his servant? Nay, verily "*As he hath
done, so shall it be done unto him.*"

Think you *the master* will escape *a whipping?* and a
whipping *within an inch of his life?* Not he. All that
he will receive less, will be *mercy, not legal justice,* ac-
cording to the law of Moses.

Nor is this all. Look at Exo. xxi. 18, 19 : The man,
who in strife (private quarrel) smites and injures another, but so that he recovers of the injury, " *shall pay
for the loss of his time, and cause him to be thoroughly*

healed." So in ver. 22 : The man inflicting injury
" *shall pay as the judges determine.*"

In the case (vs. 28–31) where the injury to a man *is
done by an ox*, the owner of the ox may *ransom his own
life*, which is forfeit, by such a sum of money as the
judges may lay upon him.

Suppose the *servant*, dying in this case, leaves behind
a wife and children, will the master escape being mulcted
in damages, corresponding to the estimated value of the
services of the husband and father, during his presump-
tive lifetime? Nay, verily.

The Mosaic law is wonderfully comprehensive and
minute in its provisions for the redress of injuries and
wrongs done to any man and every man, in whatever
situation and relation, and of whatever rank, " from the
hewer of wood to the drawer of water." And he who
flies to this law for refuge from punishment for wrong
doing, only throws himself into a " *consuming fire*," as
Jehovah declares himself to be — to all the workers of
iniquity. Exo. xxiv. 17 ; Deut. iv. 24, and ix. 3 ; Heb.
xii. 29.

The Mosaic law provides *three things* for this *servant-
whipper*, where his crime is not avenged as murder, viz. :

1. An assessment of damages, as the judges shall determine, according to the value of his services, over and
above what had been paid him, for the period of his pre-
sumptive life, for the benefit of his family.

2. *A severe public whipping*, by officers of the government, duly appointed. For it should not be overlooked,
as it often is, that *the retributions rendered* were the result of *regular judicial proceedings — in open court*. To
suppose otherwise would be to suppose a state of anarchy.
See Exo. xviii. 25, 26 ; Numb. xi. 16, 17 ; Deut. i. 15,
16, 17. Don't forget the fundamental principle in all

5

cases of judgment — "eye for eye . . . wound for wound . . . stripe for stripe." Exo. xxi. 25.

3. *The separation of the criminal from his family and house and home* — to take up his quarters in the city of refuge, *never to leave it on the penalty of death*, till after the death of the high priest who officiated at the time of the judgment. See Numb. xxxv. 11–28.

To suppose a less severe judgment by the Mosaic courts of law, is to suppose the punishments for crimes not proportioned to their character and importance, which is a charge which cannot be justly preferred against the wisdom and benevolence of that law.

"The law of the Lord is perfect;" so says David. But it cannot be made so to appear, if its provisions are inconsistent and incongruous.

If the man who killed his neighbor by the slipping of the head of his axe from the helve, *by accident*, was obliged to go to the city of refuge and stay, it may be the rest of his life — at any rate till the death of the high priest who was in office at the time of its occurrence, is the man who, *in a passion*, and *not by accident*, beats his fellow with a rod till within an inch of his life, to be permitted to stay at home in the enjoyment of the society of his family and friends? Not according to the provisions of this law.

And those who give interpretations of it, which render it incongruous with itself, or evidently unjust and unmerciful, are guilty of bearing a false testimony against God, who claims to be its author. No man will ever *willingly put*, or *allow*, a construction of a word or deed of a FRIEND, which militates against his interest or character.

The man who volunteers or allows of interpretations of the Divine law, which is a reproach to its author, and implicates his justice and benevolence, and especially his consistency, as a lawgiver, can be no true friend of God. He is as Joab to Amasa — with a kiss, and the word of friendly salutation *on his lips,* — "Art thou in health, my brother?" — *and a dagger at his vitals !* See 2 Sam. xx. 9, 10.

I have alluded, *incidentally,* to the passage in Exo. xxi. 16 : " He that stealeth a man and selleth him, or if he be found in his hand, he shall surely be put to death." A collateral passage is in Deut. xxiv. 7 : " If a man be found stealing any of his brethren of the children of Israel, *and maketh merchandise of him,* or *selleth* him, then *that thief shall die.*"

The word here rendered " stealeth," is *Gaunab,* signifying *the taking from another* what belongs to him, without his consent, it being the same word that is used in the eighth commandment, and, by commentators generally, admitted to prohibit, comprehensively, all that is involved in fraud, felony, and robbery.

The crime set forth in the two passages includes four counts. 1. The *stealing* of a man. 2. The holding of him. 3. The making merchandise of him. 4. The selling him. These four points are included under one general provision of law — they are one and all put on the same level. The man that is found guilty, under any one of the counts — either of stealing, or holding, or making merchandise, or selling — is *punishable with death. Either is a capital crime.*

It is a matter of some importance to know what shall be construed into such a crime.

The crime alleged, consists, evidently, in *taking,* or *holding,* or *selling,* some man, *without the consent of the owner.*

Who, in this case, *is the owner ?* *To whom* does the

man belong ? The associations in the minds of slave-holders and their apologists, would naturally lead them to answer, promptly, "*To some master, of course.*"

But a few grains of allowance should be made, in consideration of their circumstances, respecting the soundness of such a judgment. And, in a question involving a capital crime — life and death — we should not take *for granted*, what *requires* or *lacks proof*, *much less against proof to the contrary.*

If the owner of the stolen man had been *a master*, how easy and how natural it would have been to have said so, as there was no lack of frequency in the use of the term *master, in its proper relations.* Or if it had been *a servant* that had been stolen, how easy and natural it would have been to have used the proper word to represent the thing.

But there is nothing *here*, or *elsewhere*, to indicate, or show, that a *master* had had a *servant* stolen — or that a *servant could be stolen from any master. There is no provision of law for such an occurrence.* There is no record or intimation that such an occurrence ever took place. *But there are numerous provisions of law precluding the possibility of such an occurrence.* See pages 28–31, on the relations of servants.

In the relation given by Joseph, while in prison, of his personal history, to the servants of Pharaoh, he said (Gen. xl. 15), "*I was stolen* away out of the land of the Hebrews."

The record of this transaction, with its circumstances, is found in the 37th chapter of Genesis. The martyr Stephen (Acts vii. 9) alleges that his brethren sold him — *out of envy* — *not to make money*, though they got money for him. The major part of them, *at first*, thought to *kill* him. But Judah prevailed to modify their purpose from *killing* to *selling* him. The making *merchandise* of him was *an incident* to the general transaction, and not its object. And yet, as has been incidentally remarked, in another connection, had Joseph's brethren been under the jurisdiction and operations of the Mosaic law, their crime would have subjected them to the penalty of death.

But *from whom* was Joseph stolen? — was he previously owned by any *master?* — or was he stolen from his *father?* There is some ground to show that his *father* had some right in and to him. But the crime of *stealing him* is not composed of wresting him from his father's control. "*I was stolen out of the land of the Hebrews.*" If he had gone out of the land *voluntarily*, this could not have been said. He went out by *compulsion — by force — under constraint.* He was removed and disposed of as merchandise — *his self-ownership denied — disregarded. That* was *man-stealing*, and among the highest crimes prohibited by the Mosaic law, and punishable with the highest penalties. The restraint of one's liberty to use and dispose of himself, by another, *is the crime alleged — constitutes man-stealing* by the provisions of the Mosaic law.

One of the most eminent of the Jewish writers of seven centuries ago, Jarchi, in commenting on the stealing and making merchandise of men, employs this language : "Using a man against his will, as a servant lawfully purchased, yea, though he should use his service ever so little, only to the value of a farthing, or use but his arm to lean on to support him, *if he be forced to act as a servant,* the person compelling him but once to do so, shall die as a thief, whether he has sold him or not."

Let us look a moment at another style of evidence. In the provisions of this law, if a man stole an ox, or a sheep, and the theft was found alive in his hand, then the

5 *

thief was to *restore double*. But if the thief had *killed*
or sold the animal, he was to restore five oxen for an ox,
and four sheep for a sheep. Exo. xxii.

The penalty for stealing *property* was a *property-pen-
alty*, and a penalty of *double the amount stolen*. If the
property stolen were *a living animal*, and the thief had
killed or *sold* the property, the penalty was four or five
fold, the killing and selling being considered an aggrava-
tion of the first offence. But the penalty was always to
be paid with *the same in kind*.

Now, suppose it was *a servant* that had been stolen
from his *master;* why should not the law require the
thief, as in all other cases of theft, to restore *the same in
kind* — and double, or quadruple, in amount? Above all,
why should the law omit to provide *even for the return
of the stolen servant to his owner?*

There was no requisition of law for the return of *a
stolen man to an owner*, simply because *no owner was recognized*, besides himself, to whom the stolen man could
be returned. To return *a stolen man* to his *owner*, was
to set at liberty the man who had been held to service and
labor *against his will* — to " *let the oppressed go free*."
There was no ownership by one man of another recognized in any portion or provision of the Mosaic code.
The *pretence* of it — the assuming to act *on the principle
of it*, to the least degree, by compulsory service — was a
crime punishable with death.

One word in relation to another passage often referred
to as proof of the recognition, by the Mosaic, law of
property in man. Exo. xxii, 3 ; "*He shall be sold for
his theft*." This was a case of crime, and a case where
the thief was unable to make retribution, in *kind* or *in
money*, for the property stolen. The sale was the act,
and by the order, of the government, and of so much

time and service of the thief, as to meet the penalty of the law in such case made and provided — viz., to two-fold the amount of the property stolen. The man was then to be set at liberty.

By the provisions of this law, God has guarded the attributes of humanity — of human liberty and equality — as sacredly, and solemnly, and terribly, as Mount Sinai itself, on which the law was given, in the prohibition, "*There shall not a hand touch it, but he shall surely be stoned . . . whether it be man or beast, it shall not live.*" Exo. xix. 3.

CONCLUSION.

Without further notice of numerous other points, which naturally come up, in such a discussion, it is presumed that enough has been said, to satisfy any candid mind, that in the Mosaic law is no foundation for the idea of human chattelism — the principle of property in man.

Whoever interprets any provision of that law, into the principle of oppression, of coerced labor, of unpaid toil, of irresponsible control, above all, into human chattelism, can understand nothing of its genius, or, if understanding, must wilfully pervert its provisions.

The great Teacher and Expounder of that law, while on earth, utters this instructive and unequivocal language (Matt. vii. 12) : "All things whatsoever ye would that men should do to you, do ye even so to them ; for this is the law and the prophets."

The Savior thus asserts that the basis of all these legal provisions is kindness and good will. They *allow*, and they *require*, nothing but in fulfilment of the law, " Thou shalt love thy neighbor as thyself ; " " All things whatsoever ye would," &c.

As no man *can* desire another to oppress *himself*, or regard and treat him *as goods and chattels*, so no man can read this interpretation of the law of Moses, by Jesus Christ, *and not know* that any interpretation of it which sanctions the least unkindness and oppression, is in direct contravention of the teaching of the Son of God.

In the word of God, from beginning to end, is *not a word of sympathy* with any man, or class of men, *however associated*, who allow or indulge in the least injustice or unkindness towards any individual of the race.

God's sympathy is all against the *wrong-doer*, — the covetous, avaricious, unfeeling *tyrant*, who either *claims, uses, or justifies the use, of any man's service*, without due reward, — without an equivalent for services rendered. God's sympathy is all with the *down-trodden*, the *afflicted*, the *oppressed*. " For the oppression of the poor, for the sighing of the needy, now will I arise, saith the Lord." Ps. xii. 5. " He shall break in pieces the oppressor." Ps. lxxii. 4.

There is not a consideration in any attribute of God, — of wisdom, justice, benevolence, mercy, or truth ; not a provision of his law, moral or ceremonial ; not a precept, principle, or provision of his gospel, which approves or admits of any element in the whole system or code of Slavery.

Slavery, in all its elements and provisions, is at war with every precept of the decalogue, with every principle of the law of God and the gospel of Jesus Christ ; is a combination of all the elements of mischief, and sorrow, and woe, and crime, which it was the object of the Mosaic law, and of the gospel, alike, to subvert and prevent ; or, in the language of John Wesley, " *the sum of all villanies*."

And to make God its author, *or approver*, is to deny to him the attributes he claims.

And to worship *as God*, a being who looks with *complacency* or *tolerance* on oppression, fraud, and cruelty, is to worship a DEITY *of Slavery's creation* — not the God of the Bible.

And such worship, however sincere and honest, will be found, ere long, never to have been accredited *in heaven*, grateful soever as it may be to the HIDEOUS DEMON, to whom it is ignorantly offered.

The *Heathen*, even, know better than to *justify* the chattelism of human beings. Mohammedanism discards it. The Bey of Tunis and the Dey of Algiers, long ago, abolished it, " *out of regard for God and the honor of humanity.*" They esteemed, and declared, the *principle* and the *practice*, an outrage upon the first principles of moral government and law, engraven on the consciences of all men.

Nothing can be more painful to a Christian heart, than, *in this age, and in this land of boasted light*, to have occasion, as we have now, to show that the law of God, and the gospel of Jesus Christ, do not sanction the greatest atrocities ever committed under the light of day.

It is sad, exceedingly, to know, that *in New England*, professed ministers of the gospel have been found to volunteer their services for the defence of Slavery, as a patriarchal institution, upheld and supported by the Mosaic law, and by the gospel of the Son of God.

And, if possible, *more* sad to know, that such interpretations of the law, and of the gospel, have been, not only very extensively and cordially received, but *demanded* by the tastes and sentiments of the people.

It is upon the consideration of this state of the public sentiment, exhibited so extensively at the North, that I have been led to introduce and discuss, as briefly as I could, the first principles which lie at the foundation of all intelligent or efficient opposition to the institution and principles of American Slavery.

It is high time that Christian *ministers*, and Christian *men* — that *philanthropic* and *patriotic* men, should *understand*, and be able and ready to *define, what Slavery is,* and to show its *utter, total* incongruity with the teachings of the Bible.

If the claim to property in man, by a fellow-man (in which the principle of Slavery consists), be allowed as justifiable, foolish and vain are all protests and measures of opposition to the institution, or attempts to correct, what are called its abuses.

All the cruel *laws and usages connected with Slavery,* are but streams which legitimately flow from the overflowing fountain. Admit the *principle* of *"property in man,"* and the *system* of Slavery follows of a natural necessity. Probably no man, or set of men, under gospel light, can make a better system of Slavery than that which *has* existed, *and now exists*, in our land. A system built upon a foundation of chattelized humanity, *to be symmetrical*, can be made to exhibit no other features than those of *horrid monstrosities.* The whole thing is horrid in its inception, in its continuance, and in its final issues.

But without additional comment upon the slave system, I wish, in closing, to say a few words by way of a practical application of my text — *"Who is on the Lord's side?"*

I think you will agree with me, when I say, *evidently, not any man who occupies an equivocal or ambiguous position in regard to Slavery, or who attempts to occupy neutral ground.*

Evidently, not any man who is ready or willing to *apologize*, either for the *slaveholder*, or for the *slave system*, — who can look upon the one or the other with *approbation* or *toleration.*

The *principle — the system —* *is not to be put up with, not to be allowed, in or by the church, the pulpit, or by legislative, judicial, or executive governmental action.*

God condemns, unequivocally, the *principle,* and the *system,* its abettors and apologists. He commands, " Have no fellowship with the unfruitful works of darkness, *but rather reprove them.*"

There are no words of. comfort or consolation to be addressed to those guilty of such outrages upon religion and humanity, except the promise of a free and gracious pardon, on confession and repentance for the sin.

Any sympathy with the slaveholder, or his more guilty apologist, which falls short of a manly reproof and condemnation of the sin, is based on some other foundation than that of benevolence toward the sinner, or of fidelity to God.

To be " on the Lord's side," we must be *in sympathy with God in our hearts, in our speech, in our actions,* in all our *social, civil, political, ecclesiastical,* and *religious relations.*

If we are *ministers,* we *must,* we *shall,* obey the charge (Isa. lviii. 1), "*Cry aloud, spare not, lift up thy voice like a trumpet, and show my people their transgressions.*"

If we are *citizens, we shall,* according to the genius of our constitutional government, *use our best endeavors* to elect and secure, for the administration of the government, in every department, "*just men, who will rule in the fear of God*" (2 Sam. xxiii. 3), who will *obey his voice,* "*Loose the bonds of wickedness, undo the heavy burdens, let the oppressed go free, and break every yoke.*" Isa. lviii. 6.

Let every man, on this subject, consider and understand his *own position ;* and, as far as may be, the position of *all others.* Wherein he finds himself to have been in *error* and in *wrong*, let him *first*, and *without delay*, *put himself right*, before God, and before his fellow-men. Then let him seek, *kindly*, but *earnestly*, to right the position of all about him — all within the sphere of his influence, *within his reach, by voice*, or *pen*, or *press.*

" Let him *meditate*, day and night, *in this law*, and observe to do according to all that is written therein; and turn not from it, to the right hand or to the left." Josh. i. 6–8; Ps. i. 2.

Let him address himself to his work *courageously*, assured that *God is on the side of Freedom*, and will, ere long, " by terrible things in righteousness," vindicate the cause of the oppressed against their oppressors, whether individuals or nations.

Let those who have been hitherto in sympathy with oppression, be warned against continuance in the service and under the leadership of Satan, in his rebellion and treason against the righteous government of God; lest they become partakers in the doom of the ARCH-TRAITOR, of DEFEAT, AND SHAME, AND RUIN!

Let every man look to it, that he is in such position as to leave no ground to fear or falter, when the decisive interrogatory shall be judicially and finally put and settled, —

" WHO IS ON THE LORD'S SIDE?"

APPENDIX.

WHETHER there be occasion for the publication of a treatise like the foregoing, will be seen by what appears in the following extracts, taken chiefly from a work just published by the Rev. R. L. STANTON, D. D., Professor in the Theological Seminary of the Presbyterian Church, Danville, Kentucky, entitled "*The Church and the Rebellion*," pp. 562. The leading design of the author is to show the relations which different branches of the church and its ministers have sustained to the rebellion, and their responsibility therefor. His citations from published sermons, addresses, and speeches, abundantly sanction his position. I transcribe a few passages as specimens of what is furnished in any desired abundance.

The Rev. JAMES H. THORNWELL, D. D., of Columbia, South Carolina, in a Fast Day sermon, November 11, 1860, says, —

"The relation betwixt the slave and his master is not inconsistent with the word of God. . . . We *cherish* the institution, not from avarice, but *from principle*." p. 458.

In an address to "THE GENERAL ASSEMBLY of the Confederate States," December, 1861, Dr. THORNWELL says, —

"Slavery is no new thing. It has not only existed for ages in the world, but it has existed under every dispensation of the covenant of grace in the church of God. Indeed, *the first organization of the church*, as a visible society, separate and distinct from the unbelieving world, *was inaugurated in the family of a slaveholder*." . . . "We stand exactly where the church of God has always stood, from Abraham to Moses, from Moses to Christ, from Christ to the Reformers, and from the Reformers to ourselves." *Idem*.

Rev. STUART ROBINSON, D. D., Editor of the *True Presbyterian*, says (p. 461), —

"Now, in that civil code, divinely inspired, and under which Jehovah condescended to rule, as political head of the nation, there could, of course, be no statutes in principle contrary to righteousness. Yet the civil code of Moses permitted and regulated Slavery, *in the main recognizing the same principles of the modern slave codes of the Southern States*." . . . "The Saviour himself, who corrected whatever else was wrong in man; apostles, saints, divines, martyrs, synods, councils, philosophers, statesmen, moralists, *all accepted Slavery as being equally of God with civil government, marriage, or the parental relation*." p. 462.

Rev. THOMAS SMYTH, D. D., of Charleston, South Carolina, —

"*The war now carried on by the North is a war against Slavery, and is, therefore, treasonable rebellion against the constitution of the United States, and against the word, providence, and government of God*."

And much more to the same effect.

Rev. Samuel Seabury, D. D., of New York, 1861, on "American Slavery justified by the Law of Nature," says, —

"It is this [American] form of Slavery I propose to defend, *not by an appeal to local or positive law*, whether State or Federal, but by *an appeal to the law of Nature*, or the principles of universal justice." . . . "What age, before our own, could point to moralists that proclaim it an offence against nature to hold slaves in the condition in which Providence placed them?" . . . "Slavery might have existed, *so far as its character is concerned, in Paradise.*" . . . "But what (methinks I hear the reader exclaim), do you think there could have been *bondage in Paradise?* Pray, why not?" . . . "I see no reason why the relation of master and servant should not have existed in a state of innocence, as well as that of husband and wife, parent and child." . . . "All this, I confess, proceeds on the assumption that Slavery, or servitude for life, does no violence to nature, *but is good, and agreeable to nature.*"

The *True Presbyterian* warmly commends Dr. Seabury's book, in successive numbers of the paper, and says, —

"He argues that in this view of it, *Slavery, being a condition so closely allied to that in which our wives, our sons, and our daughters are placed, by the laws of God and man*, cannot be the degrading and hateful relation that modern abolitionists declare it to be. *There is no debasement in it. It might have existed in Paradise, and may continue through the millennium.*"

The *True Presbyterian* says, further, —

"It is certainly remarkable that the Scriptures employ this very relation to express our subjection to Christ. Believers are constantly called *the slaves of Christ.*" . . . "*The slaves of Jesus Christ love and revere their divine Master, and rejoice in their bondage; and so may a slave love and revere his human master, and delight in his service.*"

Rev. Joseph R. Wilson, D. D., of Augusta, Georgia, in a discourse to his congregation in that city, January 6, 1861, on the "Mutual Relation of Masters and Servants, as taught in the Bible," employs this language : —

"And, O, when that welcome day shall dawn, whose light will reveal *a world covered with righteousness, not the least pleasing sight will be the institution of Slavery,*" &c.

Rev. George D. Armstrong, D. D., Norfolk, Virginia, —

"With civil government, marriage, the family, and Slavery, they (the apostles) dealt in the same way." . . . "The church must labor to make good masters, and good slaves, just as she labors to make good husbands, good wives, good parents, good children, good rulers, good subjects."

Right Rev. John Henry Hopkins, D. D., *Bishop of the Protestant Episcopal Church in Vermont :* —

"The Slavery of the negro race, as maintained in the Southern States, appears to me to be fully authorized, both in the Old and New Testaments, which, as the written word of God, afford the only infallible standard of moral rights and obligations."

Albert Taylor Bledsoe, LL. D., *Professor of Mathematics in the University of Virginia :* —

"The institution of Slavery, as it exists among us at the South, is founded in political justice, is in accordance with the will of God and the designs of His Providence, and is conducive of the highest, purest, and best interests of mankind."

The Rev. Dr. Thornwell, before mentioned, in the *Southern Presbyterian Review*, January, 1861, maintains, —

" That the right of property in slaves " *is not* " the creature of positive Statute, and, consequently, of force only within the limits of the jurisdiction of the law." ... " *It is not a municipal institution* — it is not the arbitrary creature of the State — it has not sprung from the mere force of legislation. Law defines, modifies, and regulates it, *as it does every other species of property, but law never created it.* The law found it in existence, and, being in existence, the law subjects it to fixed rules. On the contrary, what is *local* and *municipal,* is the *abolition* of Slavery." ... " If there be any property that can be called *natural,* in the sense that it spontaneously springs up in the history of the species, it is the property in slaves. If there be any property which is founded in principles of universal operation, it is the property in slaves. To say of an institution, whose history is thus the history of man, which has always and everywhere existed, that it is *a local and municipal relation,* is of ' all absurdities the motliest, the worst word that ever fooled the ear from out of the schoolman's jargon.' " ... " Whatever is universal is natural. We are willing that slavery should be tried by this standard." pp. 456, 7.

The few extracts foregoing may suffice to show, what, for a time past, have been the sentiments of the leading religious teachers of the South, and some of the prominent ministers of the North, in respect to American Slavery. *It is important, however,* that the public should understand that the views above represented have been entertained but for a comparatively *brief period.*

In a religious paper, the *New Orleans True Witness,* under date of August 18, 1860, the editor remarks, —

" It is an interesting fact, that Rev. JAMES SMYLIE, an old school Presbyterian minister, *was the first person in our country who took boldly the position that Slavery was not inconsistent with the teachings of the Bible.* He was one of the first Presbyterian ministers who came to the South-west, and assisted in forming the Mississippi Presbytery in 1816. The general view *held at this time, and for many years thereafter,* South as well as North, was that *Slavery was an evil, and inconsistent with the spirit and teachings of the word of God."* ... " The sentiments expressed by our [Presbyterian] church, in 1818, *were, at the time, the sentiments of the whole country, and were regarded a pretty strong Southern document."* ... " When the sentiments of this letter [of Rev. Mr. Smylie, containing his Scriptural argument in defence of Slavery] was delivered, in 1835 and '36, in the churches of Mississippi, in the form of a sermon, the people generally, large slaveholders too, did not sympathize with him in his views." ... " *The idea that the Bible did sanction Slavery was regarded as a new doctrine even in Mississippi."* ... " *This letter was the first thing that turned public attention in the South, and especially in the South-west, to the investigation of the subject."* ... " SOME TWO YEARS AFTER the publication of this letter, George McDuffie, a Senator of South Carolina, announced similar views in Congress, and was regarded there as taking a strange and untenable position."

From the extracts preceding it can hardly fail to be seen that the witnesses in behalf of the Peculiar Institution do not agree together in reference to several important points ; some affirming that their *present position is the same that has been occupied for ages respecting Slavery,* while others testify that their position is only of recent date, — assumed since 1835.

How obvious, from their testimony, that the charges made by them against those who oppose Slavery, as having changed their position, is all gratuitous — *the change in position having been all on their side;* as, avowedly, in 1818, " *the sentiments of the whole country* " accorded with those expressed in the Protest against Slavery by the General Assembly of the Presbyterian Church.

Let us look a moment at *the genius* of this " Peculiar," " Paradisiacal," " Millenarian " institution, " American Slavery," — which, " by the laws of God and man," is placed on the same ground with the marriage and parental relations. How charmingly the following description and definition of Slavery harmonizes with the generally received notions respecting the relations of husbands and wives, parents and children !

" Slaves shall be deemed, sold, taken, reputed and adjudged in law, to be *chattels personal*, in the hands of their owners and possessors, and their executors, administrators, and assigns, *to all intents, constructions, and purposes whatsoever*." SOUTH CAROLINA Code. Brevard's Digest, 229. Prince's Digest, 446, &c.

" A slave is one who is in the power of his master *to whom he belongs*. The master may *sell him, dispose of his person,* his industry, and his labor. He can do nothing, *possess nothing*, *nor acquire* anything, but what must belong to his master." LOUISIANA Civil Code, Art. 35.

" *The slave is entirely subject to the will of his master,*" &c. Art. 173.

In accordance with the above declared principles of governmental action, the laws of Slavery *permit and authorize the master* —

" To determine the kind, and degree, and time of his labor; to supply the slave with such food and clothing only as he may find convenient; to inflict, *at his discretion*, any punishment upon the person of his slave ; to depute the same power over the slave to any agent."

" Slaves have no legal rights of property in things *real* or *personal ;* but *being 'personal chattels*,' they are liable, at all times, to be sold, mortgaged, or leased, at the will of their masters." " They cannot be parties before a judicial tribunal in any species of action against a master, no matter how atrocious may have been the injury received from him." " They cannot be witnesses *against a white person*, either in a civil or criminal cause." " The benefits of education are withheld from the slave." " The efforts of the humane and charitable to instruct them are discountenanced by law." " The trial of slaves upon criminal accusations is different from that observed in respect to free white persons, and in violation of the rights of humanity."

In the Virginia Black Code there are *sixty-eight* offences, *when committed by slaves, punishable with death*, only *four* of which offences, if committed by free white persons, are thus punishable.

By the Mississippi codes, the relative number is as *thirty-eight* to *twelve*.

In Kentucky, as eleven to four, &c.

See *Stroud's Sketch of the Laws of Slavery ;* also, *American Slave Code*, by Goodell.

Bourne's Picture of Slavery ; Slavery as it is, &c.

www.ingramcontent.com/pod-product-compliance
Lightning Source LLC
Chambersburg PA
CBHW021525090426
42739CB00007B/792